A Celebration a Day!
365 Ways to a Happier, Healthier Workplace

Scott Friedman, CSP

*A Celebration a Day! 365 Ways to a Happier,
Healthier Workplace*

ISBN: 978-0-9645212-9-2
Copyright © 2016 by Scott Friedman

Table of Contents

Preface

Celebration! It's your secret to a happier, healthier workplace and life.

For the past six years, my work has focused on how celebration can create a happier, healthier workplace—leading to greater productivity and team performance. Successful celebration engages team members. The result is greater connection and good fun. So how can one do 'celebration' right? First, let's define celebration:

Celebration is acknowledging all that is good! It's recognizing the good work that you do, the people you do it with, and the people you do it for. Celebration occurs when your 'to-do' list becomes your 'done' list. It's recognizing both the little and big milestones along the way. Celebration can simply be a quick word after finishing a task, like "Yes!" or "Bravo!" It might be a skinny Caramel Macchiato at Starbucks to reward yourself for a good meeting. Celebration is a mindset that keeps you focused on what is already working and helps you grow from there.

When doing research for *Celebrate! Lessons Learned from the World's Most Admired Organizations*, we asked our survey respondents: "What is essential in making celebration work in any organization?" The top four answers were: inclusivity, gratitude, play, and surprise.

Inclusivity – Making sure that everyone feels part of the team. Everyone wants to feel a sense of belonging. It's giving everyone a voice and the feeling that their voice matters.

Gratitude – A grateful feeling, emotion, or attitude of acknowledgment of the life we have and those that we share our life with. It's the ability to count our blessings even when we're feeling the pressure of daily responsibilities. It's being thankful and showing appreciation for those that make a difference in our lives.

Play – Living in the present moment. It's the ability to let go of anger, resentment, and emotions from the past and truly bring our best self to the task at hand. Being in this state of flow will allow humor, spontaneity, fun, and play to flourish in the present moment. How much fun is that?

Surprise – Honoring people through the element of the unexpected—surprising them with what is highest on their joy list. It's catching people doing the right things and recognizing them on the spot. The reason celebration fails in most organizations today is that it becomes stale. There is a lack of creativity or conscious thought that is needed to make a celebration special. By learning more about what motivates employees and what brings them great joy, we can creatively add the element of surprise to their lives, and what a nice surprise that is!

My first book in the series, *Celebrate! Lessons Learned from the World's Most Admired Organizations*, was all about turning on your GPS (Gratitude, Play, and Surprise). This book is a practical "how to" handbook with examples from our interviews and research on what the most admired companies are doing to keep their GPS turned on.

The book is divided into three sections: Gratitude, Play, and Surprise. The aim is to make it easier for you to find the perfect celebration for what it is that you're trying to accomplish.

This book is all about honoring those with whom you work and play. It's allowing them space to be their authentic selves. It's paying attention to what makes them happy and filling their lives with more of that. It's about taking your work seriously while taking yourself lightly. It's celebrating lessons learned with the people responsible for those lessons. It's turning on your GPS (Gratitude, Play and Surprise) and the GPS of the organization.

Through this book, you will come to understand that a healthy dose of Vitamin C—Celebration—when administered mindfully, will raise you and your organization to new levels of well-being, productivity and performance... one celebration at a time.

This book is intended to jump start your creativity and help you build a happier and more joyous workplace.

Stay healthy with a little vitamin C (as in Celebration) and turn on your GPS!

Scott Friedman, CSP (Certified Speaking Professional)

Scott Friedman

Gratitude

Superhero Parking

Designate special parking spots to the employee of the week. This is a simple, yet appreciated thing you can do for your hardworking employees.

Hallway Of Fame

Create a "Hallway of Fame".
Post photos of employees on a board to highlight their outstanding achievements.

Micro Indulge

Take time to celebrate all your little accomplishments throughout the day. Made the three phone calls you needed to make? Treat yourself to a miniature candy bar. Finished that report? Give yourself a quick high five in the nearest bathroom mirror.

Gratitude

Already Done

Put together a list of all the tasks you've already completed. This can be called your "already done" list. Celebrate your accomplishments instead of focusing on the tasks that have yet to be completed.

Flex Those Hours

If there's one reward that rises above the rest, it's flexible work schedules. Consider developing a more flexible and open work environment. The more control employees have over their time, the happier they will be. Employees will appreciate the openness and respond with working harder and more efficiently.

Perk Hours

A small yet meaningful way to show gratitude to hardworking employees is to give them extra hours during the day. Hand out "perk hours" to an employee who has shown excellence. These "perk hours" can be used to take a longer lunch or to run some errands in the afternoon.

Gratitude

Phone it in

Take advantage of the latest trends in telecommuting and reward employees by letting them work from home one or two days a week. Being able to have the freedom to take the kids to soccer practice, schedule dentist appointments, or have an afternoon walk is a nice treat.

'Call in Well' Day

Let employees take one sick day a year and turn it into a "call in well' day. Employees can pick up the phone in the morning and say, "Sorry, I can't come to work today because I just feel too good."

Clip-'N-Honor

Print up little coupon books to be handed out for good performance. The coupons can have various benefits on them such as "work from home one day this month," "get out of a task free," or "good for one free Starbucks". An appreciated employee is usually a productive employee.

Gratitude

Catered Dinner to Go

Provide a catered dinner for employees to take home to their families. Use this to say thank you for a job well done or just to remind employees that you care about them and their loved ones.

Happy Feet

Treat your helpful staff to a little reflexology session. Hire a masseuse to give employees a professional foot massage. This is especially nice for those jobs that require a lot of time standing.

Jumbo-Tron Birthday Card

On a poster-sized piece of paper, have everyone in the office write what they enjoy most about the birthday person. Present the over-sized card to him/her over a surprise lunch or break.

The Worst Piña Colada

This is an award for the person in the office who had to deal with the most difficult client or patient each week.
Treat that employee to a Piña Colada or another beverage of choice. Soon your employees will start to look forward to dealing with those difficult people.

Stepping Stone

Write a positive letter regarding an employee's accomplishments and send it to upper management. Include a copy of the letter in his/her personnel file.

Extra, Extra! Read All about It!

Publish a "Kudos Column" in your company newsletter. Invite nominations from anyone in the company wanting to brag about any other member of the company.

Gratitude

'Job Well Done' Wall

Create a space where you can display photos, memos, and other forms of recognition for those who have completed projects or who have done something especially meritorious.

Stop And Smell The Roses

Honor deserving employees by sending them a bouquet of flowers at home. Not only will your employee feel special, a few eyebrows and spirits will be raised at home.

30 Days to Win

Have each employee choose an outcome they would like to achieve within thirty days. This could be to lose five pounds, save $100, buy a new computer, stop smoking, or even learning to juggle. Have your employees pair up. One person will serve as the other's accountability buddy for the month. The role of the buddy is to encourage and cheer on his/her partner to accomplish the thirty-day goal. This will create an environment of winning and success in the office. When you are successful in one area of life, that feeling tends to spill over into other areas. You'll see a lot of high fives going around the office.

WOW!

All employees get five 'WOW!' cards a month to give to their colleagues when they 'wow' customers or other employees within the company. Cards can then be redeemed for prizes chosen by you! This encourages employees to recognize each other's hard work and successes.

Book Worm

Go to a book store with a particular co-worker in mind. Based on his/her interests, choose a book appropriate for him/her. Picking just the right book shows that you care enough to have paid attention to that person's interests or hobbies.

Get Mugged

Give out a personalized coffee mug on the work anniversary of an employee. Personalize the mug with sayings or photos that would be most meaningful to them. The funnier the saying or photos, the better the surprise!

Gratitude

Coffee Table Talk

Capture projects in photos and turn them into a
coffee table book. Give them out as a thank you
to all of your project team members.
Make it even more fun by having each
member sign the others' books.

Video Thanks

Have some fun saying 'thank you' in the form of
a video. Wear fun outfits. Use props.
Be a little silly all for the sake of a little gratitude.
Getting creative in the way you give thanks
will mean a lot to the recipient.

Di-Vine Thanks

Inspired by Vine, record a six second
'thank you' to an employee or your entire team.
It's a fun way to take creative advantage of video
and let people know that you are thinking
about them. A nice bonus is that it doesn't
take a lot of time.

Candy Bar Awards

You have a lot of room to get creative with this one. Give a 100 Grand to a person or team whose ideas are "worth thousands".
Hand out a *Nestle Crunch* to get someone through "crunch time". *Life Savers* are perfect for those "save your butt" moments.
An *Almond Joy* is good for the person who keeps the team positive. Give a Snickers bar to an employee who makes others laugh.

Take it on Home

Send a thank you note to an employee's house when extra time has been put in.
Be sure to include his or her family in the thank you note.

Use Your Head

Is your office full of sports fanatics?
Get a miniature football helmet from an employee's alma mater to display on his/her desk. Each time he/she does something worth rewarding, place a new sticker on the helmet.

Gratitude

Take a Seat—not Just Any Seat!

Reward hard workers with a special office chair with lots of built-in support for those long hours behind the desk.

A Day of Compliments

January 24th is National Compliment Day. Be sincere and give out as many compliments as possible. The more creatively you give out the compliment, the better. Try writing it on a Post-It note and leaving it on an employee's desk. Praise a hard worker in a unique way in front of fellow employees. The options are endless!

Super Uber

When you are asking an employee to work odd or additional hours, hire a driver or limo service to take the hassle out of driving. Whether it is for the employee, the kids or other family members, a free ride makes life easier. This alleviates stress for the employee and gives him/her more energy to finish the project.

Gratitude

'Ride and Groom'

Treat your staff to a special Uber trip to a nearby beauty salon for a manicure or a pedicure. This is a nice way to give thanks to your employees in the middle of a long work day.

What's Your Name, Rock Star?

Name a new product, specialty service or company process after a hard-working employee who was instrumental in the creation of an idea.

Celebrate the Little Milestones along the Way

Take time each day to celebrate your personal contributions, wisdom, and successes. Set aside two minutes to appreciate your achievements deliberately. Whether it's a happy dance in your office or a trip to the vending machine to get your favorite beverage, make time to celebrate yourself.

Gratitude

Coffee Craving

Some companies around the world give their employees access to an in-office barista. That's right! There is a barista in the office ready to whip up your favorite latte or cappuccino whenever you need that afternoon pick-me-up.

Honor the Boss

October 16th is National Bosses Day. Show your boss how much you care by decorating his or her office. Wrap a little gift that you know will be appreciated. Leave it on the boss' desk or hide it in the office.

Be a Task Master

Celebrate the fine work of an outstanding employee by taking over one of his/her most unpleasant tasks on a designated day.

I Appreciate You

The first Friday in March is Employee Appreciation Day. Let your staff know how valuable they are on this day by sprinkling their day with lots of love. Be creative through little gifts and notes or stop by a toy store and pick up some props and toys. Everyone loves to feel appreciated and recognized.

A Fine Receptionist's Reception

The second Wednesday in May is National Receptionists' Day. Throw a surprise party at your receptionist's favorite lunch spot or organize a little afternoon tea reception at the office.

Relax to the Max

August 15th is National Relaxation Day. Bring in bean bags, cushions, deck chairs, blankets, and share in a little relaxation with the staff. Treat yourself to a little meditation or an extra fifteen minutes to refresh and rejuvenate the spirit.

Gratitude

Yes, I'm Positive! :
Positive Thinking Day

On September 13th, in honor of Positive
Thinking Day, challenge yourself to spend
the day thinking only in the positive.
Every time you catch yourself thinking
negative thoughts, think about what you're
grateful for and quickly change your thinking.
This would be a good day to catch people
doing something right all day long.
If you can develop this continuous positive
mindset, you will see your life change
for the positive.

Pass the Gratitude, Please

Start a gratitude chain in the office.
Do this by telling someone what you
are grateful for that day. Ask him/her to do
the same with another co-worker and so on
and so forth. Your reward is an office
attitude full of gratitude.

Gratitude

Random Acts of Kindness

Once a month, for no apparent reason, surprise a colleague or employee with a special treat. Have managers leave token gifts on the employee's desk with a note that says, "Thanks for all the good work you've been doing. I noticed!" Gifts can include favorite candy, Starbucks gift cards, movie tickets, concert tickets, or made-up coupons offering benefits.

Cook up Some Appreciation

Let the leaders or managers cook breakfast, lunch or even dinner while the staff relaxes, enjoys, and feels appreciated. After all, the quickest way to an employee's heart is through his/her stomach!

A Note of Gratitude a Day

Before you leave the office, hand write one note of gratitude to someone in your life. With the ever-growing popularity of Facebook, Twitter, and texting, handwritten notes are rare. A handwritten note is sure to catch the attention of the recipient.

Gratitude

The 'Best of the Best'

Start off your meetings by recognizing what
is working as opposed to what is not.
Ask team members what was the best thing that
happened to them since you met last or to share
the best customer interaction they had this week.
A spoonful of the "Best of the Best" sets
a positive, grateful tone which makes the rest
of the meeting more positive.

Smile! You're on Candid Video

Set up a video camera in a spare office or
conference room. Invite employees to record a
message expressing appreciation for a colleague.
Make it more fun by providing hats, wigs,
or colorful glasses to make it easier to share
feelings. The resulting film can be used to
lend some personal flavor to the company
meeting, or as a marketing tool to show
potential employees or clients how you
honor one another in the workplace.

My Bucket Runneth over

Each employee is given a bucket or colorful container for his/her desk. Encourage employees to add to each other's bucket with little notes of thanks for the good things that they do. Managers should make it a point to keep those buckets filled with gratitude!

A 'Wall of Gratitude'

Create a 'Wall of Gratitude'. On it post photos of the people that made the company what it is today. Add stories of the founding of the company up until the present day. Every year add to the wall with what you're most grateful in that year.

It's a "Week" Excuse

Toward the end of each week, show some gratitude for a week well done with some sort of employee treat. It can be bagels with the boss on Thursdays or frozen yogurt on Fridays. Employees feel a whole lot of appreciation with these small simple treats.

Gratitude

Go Fish

During the month, have employees in
different departments write down the name
of an employee that deserves to be recognized.
Place names in a fishbowl. At the end of the
month collect papers and calculate who won the
most votes. Award a prize and celebrate
the person who had the most votes.
Draw from the remaining names in the
fishbowl for another surprise winner!

Pick a Goal, Any Goal

At the start of the month, each employee is given
an accountability buddy. Each partner declares
five goals with one being a stretch goal.
Every time, a goal is accomplished, a micro
celebration is launched. A 'YES!' with a fist
pump, high 5's or maybe even a call to your own
voice mail to brag. When the stretch goal
is achieved, a bigger celebration between
buddies ensues. A Starbucks treat, popcorn
in the middle of the afternoon or even a song
of celebration can be the stretch goal reward.

Gratitude

Welcome Home

Invite the team over to your house for a meeting. Provide a main course and have others bring a side dish or dessert. It makes the meeting more fun.

Candles and Questions

Cisco Systems Inc. CEO, John Chambers, hosts a monthly hour-long birthday breakfast for any employee with a birthday that month. This celebration allows the employees to get to know the CEO on a more personal level. Add a token gift and increase the impact.

Steal Some Chill

Set aside a quiet space or unused office in your building where employees can meditate, chill out, or even take a short nap. Giving employees the opportunity to recharge their batteries, if only for a quick minute, will increase their productivity and efficiency.

Gratitude

Breakfast is on Me
To say thank you to a deserving employee, treat the honoree to a special breakfast with an employee or friend of their choosing. Breakfast is on company time and hosted by the company.

Breakfast from the Boss
Bring in a catered breakfast for your team. Designate yourself as the main waiter, serving all of your curious staff. What a fun way to start off the day. The team will surely get a kick out of you, the boss, playing waiter or waitress.

Pay the Grump Pot
Create or provide a colorful container. Call it the "grump pot". Put a dollar in the "grump pot" for every negative comment. Have fun calling out others on their negativity. At the end of the month, the money collected goes to the most positive person of the month's favorite charity. Get creative in determining the most positive person of the month. (Ideas: Voted by employees, customer mentions, the number of times that they smile.) This is a great way to help get rid of negativity around the office and simultaneously raise money for a good cause.

Complimentary Secret Santa

For a twist on the classic Secret Santa,
have employees draw the name of
another person, but instead of giving secret gifts,
have them type one short, complimentary note
once a week for a month to the person
they selected. At the end of the month,
everyone can guess who his or her
complimentary Secret Santa is!

Office Auction just Cause

Have everyone in the office donate one item
of value from their house for the auction.
The company also donates something of
value like a weekend get-away or dinner for
two at a nice restaurant. Keep all items on
auction in the break room or conference room
with price sheets attached going for a week.
Give all the auction proceeds to a cause
voted on by the employees.

Gratitude Circle

Want to set a positive tone for a meeting or end
with one? Try a gratitude circle. Provide time for
anyone to acknowledge anyone for anything.
For example: "Barb, I just wanted to say thank
you for always looking out for me and trying
to make me look competent even when
I'm not." Do this activity often. Companies
that regularly have Gratitude Circles create
a culture of kindness.

Kickoff Party

Kick off every big new project with some kind
of pep rally. Print t-shirts, serve food, put up
streamers, create a team song or slogan, and
honor the new project in a fun way. This will
create a positive feeling toward the project.

Peer-To-Peer Recognition

Have a recognition event created for employees
by employees. Let them decide what they want
to recognize and how they want to celebrate.

Fast E-Blast

Send a note through the intranet or an email
to the entire organization explaining how
impressed you are by a certain employee
for going above and beyond.

Grati-Text

Take out your phone and send a Grati-text
(a text message that expresses gratitude)
to a person who has done something you
appreciate or an employee with
a special accomplishment.

Thank you Video

Record a quick, under-thirty-second
video on your phone expressing your
thanks to an employee or a particular
department for a job well done.
Wear or hold a prop and disguise your
voice for maximum entertainment.

Gratitude

Sweet Music

An effective way to show gratitude is to create a playlist of songs that your recipient will appreciate. Send it electronically and burn a CD for listening in the car. Keep a copy for yourself to play in the office at just the right time.

Coffee Talk

Depending on coffee or tea preferences, enroll in a coffee or tea club or ship some gourmet coffee to someone you appreciate as a thank you. My personal favorite would be Café Britt (www.cafebritt.com). If you want to thank a whole department or team, replace the regular coffee in the break room with some new gourmet flavors.

Just the Scraps, Please

Document your organization's milestones with an official scrapbook. Where do you start? How about the employee of the month and other awards? Create some clever new awards that would make good reading in the scrapbook. It's also a good opportunity to acknowledge completed projects and promotions within the company.

Company Currency

Reward employees with your own company brand of funny money (e.g. Monopoly money or gold stars). Employees can redeem this currency for gifts at the end of each quarter.
Create a system that makes it fun to reward the funny money while acknowledging good deeds accomplished. It's a great way of creating a reward culture that reminds employees that good work pays off.

The Morphing Trophy

Present a big trophy to an employee you want to recognize for the week. At the end of the week, the trophy is returned with one thing added to it. You will be amazed at how many things can stick to a trophy. Keep giving the trophy to a new winner each week. At the end of the year, you'll have a trophy with fifty-two things stuck to it placed in your reception area for all to see.

Gratitude

Magazine Madness

Give a deserving employee a subscription to his or her favorite magazine. The gift shows up monthly (or weekly) all year round as a reminder of your appreciation.

Good Memories Cards

Get each employee to write something positive about the person you're recognizing on a slip of colorful paper or on pre-printed cards. Put them all in a decorated container or frame them and give them to the person who is being appreciated.

Commute On Me

A gas card or a public transportation pass can go a long way to say thank you for all the hard work an employee is completing on the road to the company's success.

Double Dutch Time

After a big finish line is met, reward the staff
with "double Dutch time"—double the time of
their lunch or breaks for the day.

Founder's Wall

Instead of a regular space on the wall for
employee photos, create something that not
only recognizes employees with a photo,
but with a short description and timeline of
how they have contributed to where the
company is today. Make sure you leave
space to add to their accomplishments
as they keep succeeding.

Dinner With the Boss

There's no better way to get an employee's
attention than to take him/her and his/her
family to dinner. Find out dietary restrictions
and preferences ahead of time.
Keep conversation light and non-work.
Take this time to get to know the employee
and family on a more personal level.

Time Released Shopping Spree

Treat your employees to a fun shopping spree
as a way to say thanks for their efforts.
Take them to a local shopping mall, give them
$100 (amount can vary), and thirty minutes
to spend the entire amount. Play a little
show 'n tell when you get back to the office
to see what everyone bought.

"You Should be Certified"

Have employees give clever awards to
one another that can be found at a
number of different certificate sites like
www.Creativecertificates.com or
www.123certificates.com. Better yet,
create your own certificates. Try 'Happiest
Person in the Office,' 'Grouch of the Day,' or
'Busiest Person on the Planet'.
It's a fun way to honor the
idiosyncrasies of those in the office.

Honors Award

As a way to break the stress of any project, take time out to make up awards to present to each team member. Some ideas are: 'Most Likely to Stay the Latest at the Company Party,' 'Most Likely to Push the Company Dress Code,' 'Most Likely to Break in to Spontaneous Dance,' 'Most Likely to be Voted Most Likely'. Remember to be respectful while at the same time having a little fun with the personality of each team member.

Let it Go Party

At the start of a meeting, everyone declares one thing that they need to let go. It could be a belief, a negative feeling, an outdated way of doing something, or anything that needs to go. Write the item down on a slip of paper and put it in a helium balloon and tie the knot. Have a ceremony honoring the letting go of that which no longer serves you and what it will make space for in your life. Then, after a moment of silence for the behavior or belief that just died, let go of the balloons as a group.

If It Is to Be, It's Up to Me

Start Monday morning off by choosing an
accountability buddy. Share with your buddy
the biggest item on your week's to-do list and
how you're going to accomplish it.
Give each other encouragement as you set out
to accomplish the biggest item on your list.
Check in every day to acknowledge
the progress and give your support.

It Could be Worse

At your next meeting, everyone votes on the
worst problem the team is facing right now.
Then ask everyone how this situation could be
worse. Imagine anything that could possibly
make this situation more awful than it is now.
Have fun with it. Exaggerate it. Wallow in
the pity of how bad it could be. This will help
the team realize that things really aren't that bad,
for they could be so much worse!

Fruit of the Loom

A silly and healthy way to creatively honor
those in the workplace is by using fruit!
Possible awards could be the 'Top Banana,'
'Such a Peach,' or 'What a Pear'.
There is a plethora of creative ways
to use this idea to show gratitude
for your employees.

The Blessin' in the Lesson

At the end of each shift, share the lessons
of the day with your team.
Ask the employees what they are proud of.
What did they learn? What would they have
done differently?
It's a good way to bring closure to the day
and get ready for a fresh start the next.

Gratitude

Word-ly Praise

Ask employees to name three positive words that describe what they most appreciate about each person on the team. Go around the group and have everyone share the words they have selected for their team members. Capture the words that are shared about each person and track when any word is repeated. Feed each person's words into www.wordle.net and a word art image will be based on how many times the word is repeated. Frame and present the word art to each employee at your next gathering.

Mind the Family

Celebrate the personal achievements of your team like births and graduations with a creative gift. For births, how about giving a chocolate cigar or sparkling cider? For a graduation, present a $2 bill for good luck paired with a poem or quote about the next step in life like "The best way to predict the future is to create it." Change your gifts every six months to keep the ritual fresh and meaningful.

Gratitude

'Get out of Work Free' Card

To honor your employee's family, give each employee a 'get out of work free' card.

It is good for anything relating to the well-being of the family. Events that qualify would be things like: parent-teacher meetings, recitals, and children's doctor and dentist appointments. Take care of the family and watch the emotional engagement of the employee increase.

But Why?

Before going home for the week, share with your team what didn't work and why. Celebrate the reasons why and let it serve as a catalyst for improvement for the next time.

Changed My Life List

Think about all of the people that have touched your heart and have changed your life in some way. Once a week, send a note to one of these people thanking him/her for the difference that he/she made in your life.

Gratitude

Help! I Need to Thank Somebody.

Think about a recent accomplishment.
Make a list of all the people that helped make
that accomplishment happen. A handwritten
note of gratitude, a call, or a post are always
appreciated by the recipient. It's a wonderful
reminder that nobody does it alone and sharing
the praise makes everyone feel better.

What's the Gift?

For the next thirty days, look at everything
that happens in your life as a gift or opportunity
to learn a lesson. Ask yourself, after any
challenge or obstacle: What is the lesson
to be learned here? Why is this a gift?
You will learn to look at life's challenges in a
completely different light.

Promote Their Passion

Give people the chance to do what they are most passionate about. If an employee is passionate about art, give him/her a project that nurtures his/her creativity. If an employee has a passion for giving back to the community, assign the task of helping facilitate a community service project for the company. The possibilities are endless. The reward will be more engaged and connected employees.

Lift Me up Word of the Day

Start off a meeting by recognizing a unique attribute each person brings to your team. Go around the table to each employee explaining why you thought of this particular attribute and how you believe it contributes to the success of the company. It's the perfect, quick energizer that will make everyone feel good before you get into the business at hand.

Hooray for Where I'm at

Stop, pause, and acknowledge the progress you're making on your biggest project. Many times, we get so consumed with the slow pace of a project that we forget to notice what we've accomplished so far. Take a few minutes to celebrate by grabbing your favorite snack or having a miniature dance party in your office.

On Purpose

At a luncheon or afternoon meeting, ask each employee to write a slogan reflecting life purpose. Then ask each employee how the company can help accomplish his/her life purpose.

Snap a Happy

For the next hundred days, take a photo every day of what makes you happy. It can be anything from food to family to exercise. By focusing more on the positive things in your life, you will actually become happier. Keep a file of the photos and take a look whenever you need to be reminded of what's good in your life.

A Manager Minute

Once a day in the early afternoon, give one-on-one time to each employee for one minute. Employee engagement is highest when managers consistently communicate with them. Let the employee determine the conversation. Just knowing you have a direct line once a day will make a big difference to your employee.

Basket of Treasures

Based on an employee's hobbies and interests, create a special basket for his/her birthday, work anniversary, or other special occasion. For artists, consider purchasing a couple paint brushes and some fun paint colors. If they love to drink coffee, think about getting some gourmet coffees. It seems so much more celebratory when you put special treats in a decorative basket.

It's All about Me

Honor a team member by having each employee write down something positive about that person on decorated cards. Present them in a colorful container to the recipient during a meeting, dinner or an awards ceremony.

Gratitude

Ten Thank You's a Day

The power of giving thanks and showing gratitude is powerful. Consciously say, "Thank you!" ten times a day for the entire week. See if you notice the workplace becoming a little kinder.

Pick a Box

Wrap little gifts of food or fun items in different boxes and let team members choose which box they'd like when they accomplish something big! It's a great way to acknowledge the completion of a project or a job well done.

Homemade Singing Telegram

Have a member of your staff dress up as a gorilla, clown or other costume that would hide their identity. Write a little song to praise the honoree and surprise them by singing it to them at a department or company-wide meeting. The honoree will remember this recognition for a long time, especially if the staff member sings off key.

Gratitude

It's Your Day

Name a day after a star employee and
provide a lot of publicity through e-mails
and communication as the day approaches.
Encourage everyone to bring a little memento
from home to work that reminds you of the
honoree and shower them with praise
and gifts all day long.

Appreciation Jar

Employees can fill the jar at any time with ideas
on how they would like to be recognized for
their efforts. Examples include requests like,
"I want time off work!," "I want to be taken to
lunch," or "I want you to buy me a margarita."
The key is then to use as many of these
recognition ideas as possible to let your team
know that you are listening to them.

Celebrate Company Progress

Once a year in a town hall or pep rally setting,
share with your employees a progress report of
how the company is doing. Make sure to show
gratitude and give thanks for a job well done
with gifts or prizes for employees.

Gratitude

Complimentary Compliments Week

For one entire week, make it a point to give out compliments to your co-workers and those in your community. The day is not complete until at least five compliments are given. Who knows? Employees may develop the habit of looking for the best in people.

Send Them to the Showers

Every birth and wedding deserves a shower or celebration of some sort. Have a celebratory lunch, snacks in the afternoon, or a dinner where everyone gets a chance to toast the special occasion.

Three Cheers

Start the morning off with a cheer. One of my favorite cheers comes from the organization called "Sales Professionals". They begin their meetings with the left arm raised and fist clenched saying, "I'm alive!" followed by the right arm raised and fist clenched saying, "I'm alert!" Finally, employees raise both arms in the air three times and say, "I feel great!" This is a good way to start the day. Create your own office cheer.

A Pint for a Pint

Reward employees for giving blood.
How about a pint of blood is good for a pint of
beer at the favorite local watering hole.
Or if you don't like beer you can substitute
any beverage of choice. Or find another
clever way to acknowledge those who
participate in a blood drive.

Frame It

Frame a meaningful poem, a funny moment
caught on film, or an inspirational poster for a
completed project or job well done.

Talking Plaque

Buy a photo frame on which you can record
a message. Place a certificate of appreciation
inside the frame and record a 20 to 30-second
personal message of gratitude in your own voice
for the special, hardworking employee.

What's Your Cause?

Have a luncheon and give every team member the chance to talk about their favorite charity and why it is important to them. Have a drawing to pick one charity to give a donation to from the company. This is a wonderful opportunity to find out what is near and dear to the hearts of your employees.

Teach a Kid

Start a program with a local primary school and teach kids about the free enterprise system. Giving back is a wonderful way to gain positive brand awareness in the marketplace and send a message to your employees that you really care about the community.

Welcome Wagon

Every time you hire a new employee, have a luncheon acknowledging the new hire and recognizing every employee who has been with the company for a year or more. This lets the newbies know that you value your employees and welcome them to the team.

Gratitude

A Jar of Gratitude

Keep a colorful jar or box out in the open.
Encourage employees to write down one
thing a day they are grateful for and add it
to the jar. Once every two weeks, open up
the gratitude jar and start a meeting by
reading what's in the jar. This is a good
exercise to get everyone started
on a positive note.

Smile Exchange

Start the work day by finding five people in
the office to smile at. Once you've exchanged
your smiles, the day can officially start.
Eventually, the smiles and positivity will
become automatic. Smiles lead to a kinder,
friendlier work place.

Go M.A.D.

For one week, encourage your employees to go M.A.D. (Make a difference). Focus on the small gestures that make a big difference in people's lives. These small gestures may be as simple as greeting everyone you meet with a smile and a kind word—no matter how down you may feel. It may be a ritual involving a talent you have. My friend made the best coffee-covered peanuts you've ever tasted. She loved celebrating her friends and clients by giving them a little treat paired with a pick-me-up note, "Every journey needs a few nuts." If you're famous for your muffins or chicken enchiladas, go M.A.D. If you're known for your artistic abilities, or you're just ready to practice a random act of kindness, then it's your week to go M.A.D.!

Worry Box

Every time you start to worry, write down what you're worrying about and toss it in a homemade worry box. The rule is no worrying about it once it is in the box. Pick a designated time in your day to allow yourself to worry for ten minutes about everything in the box. By choosing when to worry, you'll realize you have control over your thoughts.

Tub of Candy

Place a tub of yummy candy on the desk of an employee who needs a little extra TLC (tender loving care). This will encourage others to stop by for a visit and provide that needed TLC.

Employees Assistance Fund

Provide a fund for employees experiencing unforeseen emergencies in their life. They could apply for a grant or another employee could apply on their behalf. Employees, Retried staff, and leaders of the organization could all donate to the fund. Want to increase your brand image and loyalty to your employees? This will do it!

Clear The Air

At 4 p.m. every Friday before leaving for the weekend, encourage employees to apologize to any fellow team members for their behavior that week. The weekend will be filled with good thoughts and not the regrets of one comment you made under pressure. It's a good way to leave for the day with a clear head and conscience. Don't think this gives you permission to misbehave knowing you can apologize later.

 Play

Magic Box

Keep a colorful container on your desk and call it your magic box. During the day, write down on slips of paper the things you would like to create either at work or in your life. Add them to the box. Focus on these things from time to time. Enjoy magically creating them.

Wine, Wow, Whine Friday

Consider starting with your favorite beverage on a Friday afternoon. It may contain alcohol if approved by management (that's the *Wine*). Share a toast to something that went well during the week that you are proud of (that's the *Wow*). Then share something that didn't go so well and what you learned from it (that's the *Whine*). It's a great way to celebrate what worked and learn from what didn't.

Stash the Shoes

Consider starting a no-shoes policy at the office (optional, of course) or a special 'No Shoes' Tuesday. Provide a place to put the shoes at the entry way and post a "No Shoes Tuesday" sign. This promotes a comfortable, homey feel in the office. It is sure to create extra connection among colleagues. Encourage clients to take their shoes off when they come to the office as well.

Amazing Dance Craze

Look up the latest YouTube sensation and have your office post its own version. Some examples could include *Happy* by Pharell Williams, *Gangnam Style* by Psy, or *Thriller* by Michael Jackson. Staff will enjoy making the video almost as much as they enjoy watching it later!

Hokey Pokey Break

To break up the tension of a meeting or to provide a needed break, declare a "Hokey Pokey Break" and turn yourselves around! Have everyone stand up, form a circle if possible, and appoint a "Hokey Pokey" leader. The leader starts the song and gets to choose the three body parts that each employee puts in and takes out. In two minutes, I think you'll notice that the spirit of the meeting has completely turned around.

Cooking up Some Fun

Host a cooking class at the office if you have the in-house facilities. If not, go off-site. Work with a chef to create a cooking class for busy employees to create simple, fast, and fun meals for their families. Every quarter, you could pick a new theme. Whoever is interested can sign up. The first quarter may be Thai food and the second quarter might be Italian. This is sure to be a fun bonding experience.

National Day Calendar

Not sure what to celebrate on any given day?
Check out www.NationalDayCalendar.com.
Every day you are guaranteed at least one to five
different occasions to celebrate. For example:
September 19 is National Butterscotch
Pudding Day as well as National Talk Like
a Pirate Day! Think of creative ways to honor
different holidays in the office. You can create
fun parties where you bring to the office some
quirky props and delicious food appropriate
for the holiday! The options are endless and
are sure to create some fun energy
around the office.

Superheroes

Honor your inner superhero by dressing as your
favorite superhero for the day. Act as if you had
super powers and do the things you didn't have
the guts to do before.

Play

Tiny Tee Time

Set aside an afternoon for a mini-golf tournament in the office. Have each area or department design its own hole with materials from the office. Set up a contest equipped with prizes for the best mini-golfer and the best designed hole.

Create a Space

For two weeks, allow employees to decorate their cubicle or offices in any way they desire. You could put up mosquito netting, streamers, fun cards, and photos. Encourage employees to get as creative as possible by hosting a little competition for the best design.

Post A Happy

Invite employees to bring in photos of their kids, pets, hobbies, spouses, interests, or past jobs they have held. Post these on a board. Allocate space for everyone and watch the space fill up with what matters most to your employees. It is a great way to get to know co-workers. To make it even more fun, you could provide employees with T-shirts with pictures of what makes them happy on them. Mix things up and let employees wear shorts or sandals and just be casual on any day they wear their 'happy' T-shirt.

April Showers Bring May Flowers

Adorn the office with fresh cut flowers. Flowers
have a way of brightening up even the darkest of
workplaces. Be sure no one has flower or aroma
allergies before you do this!

Release Your Inner Kid!

Once a year, allow everyone in the office to
wear their pajamas to work. Have a contest for
the best pajamas. If you sleep in the nude, you
cannot play! Serve kid snacks throughout the
day. Play kid music and have fun games like
hopscotch, marbles, Twister, and t-ball during
breaks. In the afternoon, have a brainstorming
session looking through the eyes of a little kid
with curiosity, a sense of wonder, playfulness,
and no judgment. You'll be amazed at how the
best ideas come out of this particular day.

Movie in The Park

Find out the local schedule for the closest
outdoor movie in a park or stage one of your
own in a park, side of your building, or private
yard. Plan a staff outing with families. Rent a
popcorn machine and load up on the staff's
favorite sodas and candy bars.

Water Balloon Fight

Make sure you prepare your employees for this fun event! On a hot Friday afternoon in the summer, end work a little early and have a water balloon fight at a local park. You can invite their spouses and kids for some extra fun.

Master of the Week

Encourage the staff to share their expertise on a topic unrelated to work. Once a week, have an employee host a table at lunch where you can learn from the master.
For example, Marty shares his tricks on mastering Photoshop. The next week, Kui Peng teaches the staff how to make the best brownies on the planet. It's a fun way to get to know your fellow employees on a personal level while learning something new.

Staff Mural

Put up a large piece of paper in the break room. Encourage the entire staff to add to the mural. It could include original drawings, photos, clippings, postcards, mementos from a recent trip, memories of good times with the staff, or anything creative. Proudly hang the mural in a place where everyone can see it. This is a great team-building exercise, especially if you provide food! You may even learn about some hidden talents with this project.

S'More Bonfire

Celebrate a completed project or the hard work of your staff with an evening bonfire. Invite families. Bring plenty of hotdogs for roasting and the makings for S'mores. Sing camp songs, and take turns telling favorite ghost stories.

Hats on for National Hat Day

January 15th is National Hat Day. Celebrate by having the staff wear favorite hats to work. Staff can make their own hat or go to a toy shop and pick out a fun one. In the afternoon, have a quick reception and talk about what this hat says about you.

 Play

Can't Stop Laughing Month

April is National Humor Month. Celebrate like Bank of America with a Laugh-a-Day Challenge. Everyone brings in a joke, cartoon or something funny every work day for the entire month of April. Anyone who succeeds without missing a day is rewarded with a book of all the funny things collected during that month. This is a great way to laugh all month long and beyond.

Tip of the Tiara

As a reminder to treat your staff like royalty, how about having a roaming tiara that deserving employees share week to week. Create the criteria worthy of crown status and host a quick royal ceremony every week.

Erase with Grace

April 15th is National Eraser Day. Give your staff giant erasers to celebrate this day. Remind them that everyone makes mistakes and that's why erasers were invented. Challenge them to continue to take smart risks, make a few mistakes, and good things will happen. Have each person share the one thing they'd like to erase from the past year and what was the lesson they learned from it.

Dance around the Issues

Start off each meeting or take a break during a
tense day with a popular dance favorite. A little
Electric Slide, Cha Cha Slide, Cupid Shuffle, or *Twist
and Shout* are good for picking up the positivity
and letting go of the negativity.

Hide and Seek

Remind people about the mission, vision, core
objectives, and history of the organization with
an employee scavenger hunt. Plant clues in fun
places. Challenge employees to help solve the
company history. Mix it up and organize the
teams to include people who may not work
together on a daily basis. It's a great way to
reinforce where you came from and where
you're going while building team spirit.
No time to organize it yourself? There are
plenty of companies out there who will
do this for you.

A Treat to Complete

Celebrate the completion of a project by going to a park, beach, or lake and giving away small, fun prizes to each team member to honor their contribution to the project. Some small gifts can include chocolate coins for the best budget manager, a clever coffee mug for the person who continually stayed up late for the project, or a *Nestle Crunch* bar for the one who handled crunch time the best. It's a nice way to acknowledge a project completion and build energy for the next one.

Smile! You're on Candid Camera

Leave disposable cameras around the office with the assignment to capture smiles. Post the photos in a large collage in the break room or drop them on an employee's desk with a fun note. You can do the same with digital cameras and show the photos at the next company meeting or print them out.

Play

Full Moon Party

Have a night celebration where you gather around a fire pit. Every employee writes down one to three things he/she needs to release from his/her life. One by one they go to the fire pit and put the paper in the flames and say what they are releasing and what they want to replace it with. For example, "I am letting go of smoking in my life and will replace it with a new exercise routine." After everyone has stuck something in the fire, hold hands, and a release ceremony takes place.

Books on the House

Mind Valley in Malaysia allows employees to buy as many books as they would like on Amazon as long as they share it with the rest of the staff after reading. Charles Tremendous Jones once said that you'll be better tomorrow than you were today, based on the books that you read and the people you meet. What a wonderful way to celebrate your staff by letting them learn and grow without paying a penny.

A Night at the Oscars

Fashion your annual awards ceremony after the Tony Awards or the Oscars. Don't forget the show-stopping musical performances! Allow many people to get involved and make sure to choose a funny emcee whom all the employees know and love. How about acknowledging the best trait of each employee with an Oscars award ceremony? Categories would be based on how you'd like to honor the staff. For example, "In the category of 'Always lightening things up with good humor'—the envelope please—and the winner is…"

Honor the Oscars

On the Friday before the Oscars. Have a pool. Choose who you think will win the awards for best picture, actor, and actress. On the following Monday morning, give prizes to the winners that got the most correct.

Play

Roll out the Company Carpet

If you really want to make a big deal out
of your staff, try creating a "red carpet"
(or other company color) experience. Get a piece
of appropriately colored carpet and velvet ropes.
Have each employee walk down the carpet as
they arrive at work on the first day of the New
Year—or their first day of work. You can get a
carpet runner from any discount or department
store or have a carpet company cut one for
you. Remind staff that they are all winners and
should be treated as such.

Inflatable Breaks

Keep balloons on hand for a fun competition
one afternoon. Try balloon shaving, balloon
juggling, or a balloon passing relay where you
can't use your hands. This is sure to alleviate any
pent up stress among the staff.

Serenade the Champion

Every department must come up with a song to sing to the employee of the week or month. They can pair it with a fun dance or even silly costumes. Some suggestions for songs could be *Just the Way You Are* by Bruno Mars or *What Makes You Beautiful* by One Direction. Departments can even come up with a song parody of their own! The options are endless. The point is to honor an outstanding employee in a creative way.

Lunchtime Lip Sync

Encourage employees to stay on-site for lunch by hosting a lunchtime lip sync contest! Karaoke is also a popular way to go, but with a lip sync contest, you're guaranteed more passionate gesturing knowing you can't sing, only act.

Field Day Fun

Remember in elementary school when you had an entire day dedicated to fun outdoor games and contests? Consider hosting a company field day. Possibilities include a fun obstacle course, three-legged races, a relay race, egg tossing, horseshoes and many other imaginative ideas. Let staff suggest some competitions.

Back to the Future

Set your clocks forward because today it is going to be the year 2415 in the office! Let your imagination go wild about what to wear and how to style your futuristic hair. Use this as an opportunity to take a close look at your outdated policies and brainstorm some ways you and your staff can take the company into the future with relevancy.

Color My World Day

Pick a color, any color. On a designated day, everyone in the workplace is encouraged wear that color. It's simple. It's fun. It creates a team synergy without a lot of work.

Play

The Cleverest Workplace Ritual

How about having a contest for the cleverest workplace ritual? From a secret handshake in the hallway to a pre-meeting cheer, there are endless ways to cleverly connect, honor, and play with your team.

Go Green Day

Wear green and celebrate being environmentally conscious. This is a good reminder to honor your organization's green agenda and challenge you to take it to the next level.

Celebrate the King

To help kick off the New Year in style, how about celebrating the King! On January 8th (Elvis Presley's birthday), blast your favorite Elvis tunes in the office and encourage your colleagues to sport white jumpsuits with sequins and rhinestones. How about bringing in some banana pudding for an afternoon snack? That was Elvis' favorite dessert! This may be the only day of the year when you have permission to shake your pelvis.... for Elvis.

We've Got Spirit, Yes We Do!

Create some friendly competition by wearing your favorite team's jersey the Friday before or the day of the big game. Make some fun bets such as having the losing team's supporters agree to cook burgers or buy lunch for the winners. You can even have a tailgate party in the parking lot for breakfast or lunch to heighten the excitement.

The Nerd Herd

Spur on your inner nerd. For one day, everyone is allowed to be a nerd. Put on your thickest glasses, an old sweater from your grandfather, your mother's bobby socks, or pants that are WAY too short. Wear things that don't match, don't fit or that are out of season or style or all of the above. If this is just another day at the office for you, you'll feel right at home!

Play

Got Talent Competition

A special celebration that engages employees and creates a lot of fun throughout the many offices of Standard Chartered Bank is "SBC's Got Talent". This event gives each employee a chance to show off often surprising talents. You can imagine the excitement that erupts when the gang realizes that quiet Suzanne in the back office can belt out a soul tune to rival Beyoncé, or that timid Steve can make a guitar wail Van Halen-style. Stage your own workplace "Got Talent" competition.

Co-Worker Trivia

Test your employees' knowledge of their fellow employees by hosting a trivia event with questions about people who work at the company. What a great way to get to know your co-workers on a different level which could lead to some nice customized surprises in the future.

Good Fortune

Appoint a good fortune committee who will scour the web for the best inspirational quotes, put them on little slips of paper, and add them to workplace fortune cookies. Get creative on making your very own brand of delicious fortune cookies.

Treat Tuesday

Think about celebrating 'Treat Tuesday' on every Tuesday between Thanksgiving and Christmas. Match up departments or people who don't normally work together and assign them a day to provide healthy and/or scrumptious treats for the other groups. It's a great mixer, an opportunity to show off hidden culinary skills, and a morale builder.

Halloween Costume Contest

Provide awards for the scariest, best, and the most creative costumes. Have a little reception in the afternoon, provide festive treats, and play some scary tunes! Consider delivering candy to a kids home or go help out at a soup kitchen in costume.

Play

Treasure Hunt

Honor the newest member of the team by having a treasure hunt through the different departments. In each department, something is hidden that will teach the team members about the people in this department. Do you remember how much fun treasure hunts were as a kid? Continue the celebration by having a treasure hunt in the office. Who knows? Someone may even find the stapler that's been lost for months!

Balloon Hockey

Set up an exciting game of in-office balloon hockey to break up a long, tense day. Use long balloons for the sticks and a small round balloon for the puck. Rearrange your workspace for safety and let the games begin.

Multi-Task Juggling

April 18th is International Juggler's Day. It is the perfect day to honor the juggling of our many responsibilities we have on any given day! Bring in juggling kits and learn how to juggle! You can also juggle any three objects around the office. End the fun with some snacks and a thank you for all the juggling employees do around the office.

Celebration Calendar

Post a celebration calendar in a common area and encourage each employee to add one micro-celebration. From a day to wear their favorite color to a hat or pot-luck breakfast, the calendar slowly starts to fill up with these micro-celebrations. Be sure to hold a few celebrations off the calendar for surprises. Don't be afraid to celebrate spontaneously at any given moment.

You've Got Inspirational Mail

Every one draws a name in the office. Every day for a week each employee sends that person one inspirational quote or passage. The purpose is to create more positivity around the workplace, thus raising the spirits and productivity of the entire staff.

Surprise... You're The Host!

Every month draw a name from your department. That person gets the high honor of hosting lunch. They get to choose a lunch place close to the office and even the topic of conversation. Once a name is drawn, that person isn't eligible again until all names are drawn.

A not-so-Radical Sabbatical

Go to a park, beach, or a nice place by a stream with your department or team. Let each person talk about the support they need to reach peak performance. By asking for help and stating what needs to change in their life to achieve better performance, the wheels are set in motion to accomplish this.

A Beach within Reach

You don't have to drive a distance to get to the beach to host a party. Instead, bring the beach to you. Have an afternoon beach party in the parking lot or an open space close to the office. Wear beach attire. Bring your beach balls, sandals, and anything "beachy" to make your experience more authentic.

Sing Your Complaints

Invite workers to complain, but, in order to do so, they must sing their complaints to the tune of their favorite kids' song. It's a very quick way to realize that your issues are just not that big a deal when seen in the light of a kids' melody.

It's about to Get Ugly

Sponsor an ugly tie contest for men and an ugly scarf contest for women, or have an ugly sweater contest for all employees. On this particular day, everyone has a chance to dig through their closet for the ugly! Be sure to take pictures! After the winner of the ugly tie or scarf or sweater contest is awarded, put those ugly things in a box to donate to Goodwill or Value Village or Salvation Army. Post the pictures on an office wall or bulletin board to remind employees to have fun at work.

Celebrate Today in History

Log on to www.holidayinsights.com and get creative about how you want to celebrate this day in history. For just about every day of the year, you will have choices of what to celebrate that has happened in the past. It's up to you to decide exactly how you want to celebrate—get creative!

Kazoo Applause

Hand out little kazoos to your team and have them acknowledge every completion on their to-do lists this week with a little kazoo applause. It's a wonderful way for everyone to share in the celebration!

Bring Your Child to Work Day

Invite employees' children to come to work with their parents. Have cereal and cinnamon toast and share cartoons in the break room for this special day. Have candy and kids' snacks available throughout the day. For afternoon breaks, provide children's games such as "Pin the Tail on the Boss," sing-along songs, and even pillow fights. Let kids spend the day seeing what their parents do at work.

Bless Your First Stress

Celebrate your first stress of the day, whatever it may be! Did you have some early morning computer issues? Bravo! Time for a latte and a chocolate croissant. This little ritual will remind you that stress is not an event. It is just one's perception of an event. We have control over our emotions.

Prop Up Your Meetings

Have a selection of funny headpieces, masks, wigs, animal noses, fake mustaches and other fun props available for staff meetings. It will be a constant reminder not to take ourselves too seriously, no matter how serious the situation may appear.

Charade Parade

Need to solve a problem or kick start the creativity of your group? A quick game of Charades to start a meeting or a project may be your perfect answer. You'll immediately engage the right side of the brain, and before you know it, the cleverness will trickle over into your problem solving. Other possible games include *Cranium, Pictionary,* or *Scategories.*

Canvas and Cocktails

Bring in a local artist or a self-proclaimed artist from the staff to teach an art class for the group. You can provide virgin cocktail drinks (or alcoholic if approved by management) and hang the art up in the hallways after class. This is a fun activity that is sure to get your staff thinking creatively.

Exercise the Right to Exercise

Start a contest for those who want to get healthy and/or lose a few pounds. You can play for lunch sponsored by the person with the fewest amount of kilos lost or you can raise money for a cause and every kilo dropped means money for the cause. Endorphins and good energy will definitely flow around the office.

Honor the Awkward Award

Almost everyone has a school picture from their awkward years tucked away somewhere. Invite everyone to bring in their most awkward picture from their younger years. Have a contest for the "Most Awkward" and "Most Improved". Everyone gets one vote for each category. This is a good way to laugh at ourselves and connect with our co-workers.

Spring Into Cleaning

Make a celebration out of cleaning up. Have employees bring in their favorite breakfast snacks or lunch creations. For thirty minutes, everyone takes part in cleaning out and off their desk and cubicles. Play some upbeat music, dance a little, and clean a lot!

Play

No-Brainer Day

February 27th is No-Brainer Day. That's the day that you get a chance to take it easy. Celebrate those tasks that are simple, easy, obvious, and don't challenge the mind. Since you're taking it a bit easier than usual, it's also a great time to reflect on the more challenging tasks that you've completed recently and treat yourself to a little something special in their honor.

Meet Me in the Middle

March 10th is Middle Name Pride Day. Have the employees wear name tags with their middle name proudly displayed in honor of this special day. Have fun teasing each other and coming up with new slogans and nicknames using your co-workers' middle names.
If you don't have a middle name, you get to choose your very own nickname for the day. It's a good way to connect with your co-workers in a different way.

Play

May I Suggest?

For one week, put out a suggestion box asking for ways to bring more celebration into the organization. At the end of the week, have a celebration committee choose the best idea to be implemented. Create a campaign or rally around the new idea and get everyone excited about your new celebration ritual.

Mini Me T-Shirts

Collect baby photos from everyone in the department and have them made into t-shirts. At the next retreat or meeting, have everyone wear their t-shirts showing off his/her baby photo. It will remind us to honor the kid in each one of us and be more curious, spontaneous, and playful even at work.

Each One Teach One

Once a month, employees can request to have lunch with another employee who is an expert at something that they would like to know more about. For example, Ramesh is an Excel whiz. For the price of a salad, you can ask him anything you want about using spreadsheets. Your staff continues to grow and learn while experts feel good about teaching others.

Play

Let's Go Fly a Kite

Have a play hour once a month where employees meet at a local park and fly kites, play volleyball, croquet, horseshoes, or badminton. It's a nice break in the month and employees look forward to having a little outdoor fun.

Opera Day

When things are bad at work, sing to each other for a minute or two about your work challenges in falsetto or your very best opera singer imitation. Troubles never seem so bad when they come out in song. Plus, hearing your co-workers attempting to sing opera will be a hoot! Who knows, you could even end up finding some real talented singers in your team!

Once-a-Week Joy

Write out a list of all of the things that bring you joy. Keep the list close so you can continually remind yourself of these activities. Set a goal to engage in at least one activity on your "joy list" each week. All work and no play leads to a decreased sense of celebration and joy. Smile more. Gain more balance in your life by honoring what is on your "joy list."

Play

Turn on the Funny

Jump start your creativity by watching a comedian, humorist, or your favorite funny video before doing a brainstorming session. Studies show creativity increases after watching something humorous.

Sixty-Second Revival

In the middle of a busy or tense day, blow a train whistle and hold a sixty-second revival meeting. Employees all gather in a central place to lead a cheer, sing a song, or share in a quick snack. Employees go back to work feeling revived and energized.

Un-resolution

In the first week of the New Year, make a list of the things that you are going to stop doing. Share it with your colleagues. You can post it on a bulletin board, the company intranet, or share it through a Facebook or Twitter or Instagram. Peter Drucker, a management guru, reminds us that most leaders know what to do. What they need to know is what to stop doing.

Play

Smile across the Miles

Make it a point to flash a big smile to every person you walk by today. Make it one of those smiles where it looks as though you've just won the lottery. See how people respond to you. You will find that life is a mirror and that most every smile will be returned with another smile.

Push the Drinks

On the last Friday of the month, have one of the newer employees push a drink cart throughout the office spreading good cheer while getting to know his or her colleagues. Whether it's cream soda or something a little stronger, it will make for a spirited afternoon. It's a great way to celebrate special events like St. Patrick's Day, Cinco de Mayo, Chinese New Year, Independence Day, or any other holiday.

Dance to the Weekend

Appoint one person to collect YouTube clips of popular songs throughout the week. On Friday afternoon, bring the entire staff together for a fifteen-minute dance party using these clips. It's a great start to the weekend.

Trash Can Basketball

On a Friday afternoon, invite employees to write down three stressors of the week on three different sheets of paper. After all the stressors have been written down, have employees wad them up and take turns shooting them into a trash can fifteen feet away. Hand out prizes for employees who make all three baskets. The purpose of the exercise is to remind people not to take their stress home with them for the weekend. This is a symbolic gesture to let go of all the stress before the weekend starts so that you can enjoy your family and weekend festivities.

Jump for Joy

Grab all of your staff to participate in a standing long-jump competition. Have each person start at the same spot in an open hallway or room and have them jump as far as possible from a standing position. Mark each participant's jump length with a strip of masking tape on which is written his or her name. Whoever jumps the furthest wins a prize! Remind employees that it's okay to jump ahead, but let's not jump to conclusions!

Common Circle

Form a circle with your employees.
Pick a person to start. This person makes a
statement about a favourite thing or a fact
about his/her background. The person could
say, "I like Chinese food." Then, everyone who
likes Chinese food joins the circle. A member
in the circle then shouts out another fact or
interest. This person could say, "I grew up in
the Midwest." Everyone who grew up in the
Midwest joins the circle. Play for ten minutes
at a time. It's a great way to learn more about
the interests and hobbies of those that
you work with.

Flip Flop Day

Set a short-term goal for your team or
department. When it is accomplished, the next
day is flip flop day. On flip flop day, everyone gets
to be casual and wear their favorite pair of flip
flops or other creative, casual footwear.

Play

Field Trip

Take your employees for a tour of one of your vendor's or supplier's facilities. It's a cool way to learn more about your suppliers and fellow employees. The event is even better if you rent a bus and play games or do a sing-along on your way to the facility.

Music My Way

Honor your employee of the month by letting them choose the music in the cafeteria or facility for one full business day. Cross your fingers that their musical tastes aren't too offensive to anyone else in the office.

Show and Tell

Set aside one day a month for "show and tell". Have lunch catered. Encourage employees to bring in something from home to "show and tell" other employees about. It doesn't have to be a trophy they won, just an interest such as a cake recipe, a new video game, or a cool memento from traveling.

Play

Family Day

Set aside one afternoon a year for employees to bring in family, kids, or friends for a pizza party or other activity. Set up tours of the company so their family can see where they work and what they do. Employees will feel appreciated and you can get to know their loved ones.

Team Sports

Join a league with fellow employees. It doesn't matter if it's summer softball, bowling, or badminton or something unusual like breakdancing, dragon boat racing, or synchronized swimming. The idea is to build relationships, camaraderie, and respect among employees.

Superhero of the Week

Pass the Superman trophy please! Every Friday, vote for the person that overcame the week's toughest villains and prevailed with those superhero powers. It's a fun way to recognize and reward overcoming obstacles.

Experiment Day

Google is known for their "Twenty Percent Practice". It gives engineers twenty percent of their work time to pursue Google-related projects that they feel personally invested in. One day a week, engineers can sweep their desks of everything at the top of the company's to-do list and engage with the project they are most excited about.

Ideas like Gmail, Google News, and employee shuttle buses have their roots in this twenty percent time. Consider adapting this practise for your own employees and give them a chance to work on what they are most excited about that benefits the company.

Toss it Tuesday

You can do this as a department, team, or company depending on the size of your organization. Start with a mixture of fresh greens. Everyone brings in a favorite salad ingredient enough for at least 80% of those participating. Not everyone will like every ingredient. The Head Salad Master for the day makes a toast with an inspirational quote, story, poem, or funny anecdote. Afterwards, everyone makes their own salad with their favorite ingredients. You can have an agenda while you're eating or just enjoy conversation. It's an inclusive team-building exercise and a healthy way to have some fun together.

Culture Club

To celebrate the holidays of different nationalities or just to honor the diversity of staff, Mind Valley of Malaysia hosts culture days. On these days everybody dresses up to honor that culture. You may borrow a Sari from an Indian friend for a Deepavali/Dewali celebration or traditional Chinese Costume for Chinese New Year. What a nice way to create the spirit of inclusivity at your work place and make everyone feel valued.

An Inspired Lunch

Share lunch together. It could be potluck or brown bag. While eating, ask the group what books they have read, plays or movies they have attended, museums or art galleries visited, or other experiences they have enjoyed lately. Ask the group to brainstorm how those experiences can inspire innovation in the organization. You never know what great idea will come out of it.

Office Olympics

Celebrate the Olympics by hosting your own version of Office Olympics. Choose teams based on country, region, or whatever makes sense and get in the spirit! Start with some sort of opening and closing ceremonies. Each day host one fifteen-minute event. Activities could include trash basketball, office chair obstacle course, paper airplane, toss for distance and accuracy, and whatever else your creative mind can come up with. Make up medals and have some good, competitive fun.

Play

Camp Songs

Recall your favorite camp songs. Take an afternoon break to teach your team or department the words and the motions of the song. It's a nice way to take a quick break from the demands of work and remember the good ol' days.

Stand up and Dance

Every time you hear a certain song on the radio, everyone must get up and dance for fifteen seconds. It's a fun way to take a spontaneous break. It keeps things light and engaging. This is also a wonderful game to play at home. My friends, Elizabeth and Stephen, dance every time they hear the love song they heard on their very first date.

Autograph Bingo

Have one person go around the office collecting extremely unique facts about everyone. One day, give everyone a bingo card with the list of these very unique facts like "Got stranded in the Des Moines airport one Christmas." Employees have to find the person that matches these facts. The first person to fill out the card wins. It's a great way to learn interesting facts about those with whom you work.

Pop This

Right Selection in Dubai organizes seminars and training programs and distributes great books. They keep their staff motivated with a process costing pennies. The General Manager, Gautam, writes, "At the beginning of the month, we distribute six colorful balloons to each staff member in the office. Each time any staff member receives good news—over the phone, fax, or e-mail—he or she blows up a balloon and pops it with a loud bang. Everyone notices and asks what the good news is. This spreads news quickly throughout the office. The first person to burst all six balloons each month wins dinner for two. Then we restart the process with six new balloons each and another free dinner to be won."

This creates a lot of anticipation for good news, followed by excitement and communication each time someone bursts a balloon.

Points for the Unpleasant

When an unpleasant task comes up, reward the person that does it with points redeemable for prizes. Points for the task are based on how unpleasant the task is. It will make it more fun and easier to ask employees to do that which they may not want to do.

Senseless Question Week

Come up with crazy questions all week and give prizes for the funniest question. Examples include: Why is abbreviated such a long word? What's another word for Thesaurus? Do cannibals not eat clowns because they taste funny? Do vegetarians eat animal crackers? If the cops arrest a mime, do they tell her she has the right to remain silent?

Turkey Trot

During the week of Thanksgiving, give a prize for the best "turkey" story. Turkey stories are when you did something foolish that may still cause you to blush when you relive it today. Laughing at yourself and letting others laugh at you can be like good therapy.

Play

Name that Tune

Have one employee put on a pair of headphones and pick a song. He/she listens to the song and sings along using only la-la-la to the tune of the song. The first one to guess the song wins a small prize or coffee on the boss.

Colorful Solutions

Cover the conference table with white paper. Give everyone colored pencils or crayons to draw out the solution to the problem at hand. Then have people guess what the solution is based on the drawing. It's a fun way to solve problems without getting too intense.

A Funny Mission

Have a contest where employees recite the company mission statement using their best impression of a famous actor, a funny voice, or to the tune of a nursery rhyme. It effectively reinforces what the company stands for.

Starting Day Caricature

Root Learning in Sylvania, Ohio creates caricatures of employees when they join the consulting firm. As the years go by, coworkers add details to each drawing reflecting the employee's interests, quirks, and their innovative contributions to the job. As the pictures evolve, they reflect a growing understanding of the individual. On the eighth year, a personalized background is added by a company artist.

It's about Time Rewards

Turn any task into a game by giving yourself or your team rewards for finishing within the allotted time. If you complete the report by 3 p.m., you get dinner and dessert. If you finish by 4 p.m., you just get dinner. If you finish at 5 p.m., only snacks are awarded. Have some fun with the finish lines you set for you and your team.

Video Scavenger Hunt

Give teams a chance to engage in videography.
List five scenes that every team has to film
in order to qualify to win. Share the funniest
scenes from each team at a banquet or your
next meeting. Examples include: Film a scene
on stage with a band. Film a scene with a police
officer. Film yourself reciting the company
mission statement with three pieces of fruit.
Get creative and have some fun. This is a great
bonding experience for the whole office.

Happiest Person of the Week Contest

Once a quarter, host the happiest person of
the week contest. Give a surprise to the winner.
Get creative about the criteria for your
team or workplace and watch the mood
of the office improve.

Traveling Teddy Bear

Buy a fun, furry stuffed animal that will serve as your company mascot. Every time an employee goes away on holiday, they take the little furry mascot with them for photos. Upload the photos to the company WhatsApp group, Instagram, or Facebook page. Give prizes for the best use of the furry mascot.

Cookie Bake Off

Have cookie wars where employees get the chance to make their favorite cookies and bring them in to work. Everybody gets to vote for their favorite cookie. Prizes go to the person voted best cookie maker.

I'm Puzzled

Buy a big jigsaw puzzle. Keep it in the coffee room or the employee cafeteria. Encourage employees to add a few pieces a day whenever they need a little break. Choose a puzzle that is inspiring, sends a message, or is the answer to something that may be puzzling at work. Give clues along the way and make it fun to complete.

Play

Spring into Life

Bring a bouquet of spring flowers or a flowering plant to the office to spread the feeling of springtime into your cubicle or office. It could be used as an award for any behavior you want reinforced such as the happiest person in the morning or the employee who smiles the most.

Happy Morning

Starting off with a happy morning increases the chances that you are going to have a happy day. Begin the day at home with your favorite kind of inspirational music or an uplifting video. Once at work, share your ritual with the team or create another happy ritual for the office.

Title Insurance

Want to ensure a happier work environment? Let employees change their titles! Today is the day they create a brand new title for themselves. Instead of being the HR Manager, get creative and think of a new name. Some examples include Chief People Pleaser (CPP) or Head of Team Smiles. Mine is Chief Celebration Officer!

Bringing Back the Valentine

Remember those elementary school days when everyone made little Valentines for the rest of the class? It's time to bring the tradition back. Have each team member bring in Valentines for the rest of the team and include a note of appreciation on the back. Candy hearts aren't a bad idea either on this special day.

New Place in Town

Stay on top of the new hot spots in town and host a gathering to acknowledge whatever good is happening that week. Suggest that the team go together as a group in order to create some bonding experiences.

Brighten up the Corner where You Work

Studies show that brighter colors in the workplace make for a more cheerful workforce. Brighten up your work environment by encouraging employees to add some color to the office by bringing colorful things like flowers or bright pictures.

History Lesson

Serve lunch or ice cream to the staff and share some history of how the organization got started. Tell about where the company came from and where you're heading. Praise the employees for being a part of the journey and let them know what a big part of the future they are.

Frame the Team

Start with a canvas suitable for framing and some colorful paint. Have each team member put his/her handprint on the canvas along with a favorite photo involving at least one other team member. Create a masterpiece and frame later to commemorate the completion of a project.

First Friday day of Learning

The first Friday of the month at Mind Valley is designated a day of learning. Each employee brings a book or chooses one from the vast Mind Valley Library to read and learn or teaches another employee a skill that would be helpful to their life. Invest in the growth of your employees and they will invest in you.

Play

Kids' Theater

Inspired by "Tonight Show" host, Jimmy Fallon, have the kids of your team members look at the mission statement of your organization and think of three objectives that would lead to the completion of the mission statement.

Take a look at what all the kids thought. Discuss how you can achieve these desired objectives. This exercise is not only hilarious but also productive. Children have a very unique way of solving problems. They may get your team thinking more creatively.

Bite Your Tongue

Have a contest with employees for six weeks. Employees cannot raise their voices or put down another employee in any way. If they do, they are out of the drawing. At the end of the six-week period have a draw of those still in the running for movie passes and dinner for two. Hopefully most of the employees will still be in contention. The goal is to teach all employees the importance of respect and how damaging it can be to yell at or belittle another employee especially in public.

Scott Friedman | **99**

Play

Caught in the Act

Get your employees involved in catching people doing something right. Have a traveling trophy that starts with acknowledging someone for a job well done. Now it's up to that person to catch someone else doing something right within one week and so the ritual continues. It helps people focus on the good work others are doing and not on all of the challenges.

Nonsense Karaoke

As seen on the "Tonight Show" with Jimmy Fallon, take a popular song and make up nonsense words for it. It's a fun activity to do at a Town Hall meeting, annual picnic, or even during an afternoon break.

Pick a Motivator

Every employee is motivated by something different. The key is to find what that is for each employee. Ask each employee the reason they get up and come to work every day. What drives them the most? Pay attention to what they mention. Build your incentives around that.

Play

Share That Vision

In under thirty seconds, have each employee share in just a few words what the mission means to them. It's a fun way to help bring the mission statement to life and remind the staff what the organization stands for.

Cute Baby Contest

Have everyone bring in one of their baby pictures. Post all the photos on a bulletin board in the office. During the week, employees get a chance to match the baby photo with the employee. The person who guesses the most right, wins a prize. It's a fun way to recognize and celebrate something we all have in common: our childhood.

Pull An All-Nighter

Throw an innovation celebration by having a late night pizza and beer party. www.Box.net, a software company in Palo Alto, CA, hosts all-night brainstorm/hack-fests for its employees. Any idea is encouraged with beer and pizza. The following day, the ideas and stories from the night before are highly praised and the best ideas are adopted for the product. This is a really fun and rewarding way to think like www.Box.net.

Promotion Parade

When someone in the company is promoted,
blast their favorite song throughout the building
and start a promotion parade or conga line
traveling throughout the building.
Why not serve a snack after the
three-minute parade?

Celebrations Committee

Form a team from all different departments to
plan the fun celebrations for the company. This
can be anything from day-to-day surprises,
big annual events, social hours, or even little
acknowledgements along the way.

Pie Face

During the week before Thanksgiving, invite
employees to bring in their favorite pie and
enjoy the sampling of different tasty delights.
Mix and match as everyone gets to take home
some left over pie to their families. It's a great
way to encourage a grateful Thanksgiving.

Play

Desk-ercise

Bring in a boom box. Every afternoon at
3 p.m., play *I Like to Move It, Move It* loudly and
encourage employees to do some silly stretching
and movement. It works for the
Lane Crawford Joyce Group of Hong Kong.

Employees Just Gotta Have Fun

January 28th is National Fun at Work Day
and April 1st is International Fun at Work
Day. These days present your best opportunity
to put to good use all the ideas in this book.
Think about how you can make the best use
of these mandatory fun days!

If You Only Knew

Get out of the office to somewhere more
comfortable and make sure you bring some
snacks. Form a circle and give each person
three to five minutes to answer the following
statement: "If you knew this about me,
you would better understand me as a member
of this team." It's not about making excuses
for what doesn't get done. However, it's
about understanding more about your
fellow co-worker and the motivations
behind what they do.

Match the Mood to the Music

Play themed music to match the tone of your
upcoming meeting. To prove you can conquer
a challenging project, play the theme song
from Rocky or Chariots of Fire. To celebrate
an amazing team accomplishment, play Tina
Turner's *Simply the Best*. To make it through
tough times, how about blasting Gloria
Gaynor's *I Will Survive*.

Play

Most Memorable Memo Monday

Make up Monday morning memos with a positive spin. Then vote on the memos that will become mandatory. A positive memo could be that all employees must smile broadly whenever they cross another employee wearing red.

Speak up for Wellness

At the start of the month, have each team member declare a wellness milestone they would like to reach by month's end. Encourage each other throughout the month as employees strive for wellness. End the month with a big celebration honoring those that achieved their wellness goal. Support from your work community is a great motivator.

Take the Icy Plunge

On a hot summer day, encourage employees to bring shorts and t-shirts to change into and then, for a good cause, have everyone go through the ice bucket challenge together. Dump a bucket of ice cold water on each other and make a company donation to ALS or another charity of choice.

Lemonade Stand

Take a stand to honor a hard week's work by providing surprise popcorn and lemonade during a busy time. Afternoons are always more joyful and less stressful with lemonade and popcorn.

Laser Focus

After a big project or to a kick-off a new project, take the staff out for an afternoon of laser tag. Get into the competitive spirit by offering a prize to the winning team.

The Happiest Hour

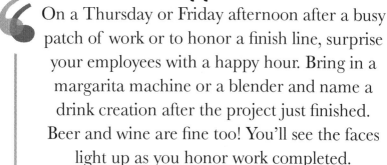

On a Thursday or Friday afternoon after a busy patch of work or to honor a finish line, surprise your employees with a happy hour. Bring in a margarita machine or a blender and name a drink creation after the project just finished. Beer and wine are fine too! You'll see the faces light up as you honor work completed. Don't forget to include nonalcoholic drinks.

Surprise

Recognize a Rock Star

Try this idea from Hyatt Hotels: Paint or decorate a small rock that will be the official "rock" star award. Each employee gets to recognize a rock star that has made a difference in some way with the presentation of the rock each month. Once they have nominated this person, two positive things happen: the employee gets surprised on their shift by other employees and all rock stars get to attend a special rock star lunch in their honor hosted once a quarter by the GM or CEO.

Fruitful Surprise

Go to the grocery store and pick out some fresh fruit or other delicious treats personalized to the desired tastes of the recipient in mind. Put the delicious treats in colorful baskets and design a specialized gift to give to the employees after finishing up a project or as a special employee recognition event.

You are Special because...

Celebrate someone in the office by having each co-worker write a note that begins with "You are special because…" and plaster the person's office or cubical with them. Their happiness and satisfaction will get a great boost that will last until the sticky notes fall off.

Concert Surprise

Surprise an employee with tickets to her favorite artist's concert. If at all possible, see if the artist will give a shout out to the employee during the concert. You could even consider getting them backstage passes to meet the artist. This shows the employee how much you care about him/her because you not only remembered which artist they like but also bought them tickets to see the artist live!

Singing Telegram

Hire a singing telegram or barbershop quartet to serenade your honored guest. This is a fun way to recognize an employee and show gratitude. If you want to save money or just be creative, have another employee dress up in costume and be the singing telegram or the quartet.

Surprise

Personal Assistant's Assistant

Have a floating personal assistant in your office
for a few weeks. Surprise different employees
with the use of a personal assistant for the day
or even for a few hours. This is a handy award
to honor the hard work of your employees.

Spic And Span

Surprise a busy employee with a cleaning
service for his/her home. This could be a
one-time cleaning or multiple cleanings
over a period of time.

M&Ms

Order customized M&Ms or Conversation
Hearts for the office or an individual.
You can choose the specific colors and message.
It's a creative and fun way to personalize
any occasion.

Surprise

Time to Get away

For the bigger milestones and accomplishments of great feats, how about awarding employees with a surprise weekend away? Everyone involved packs a bag for a weekend away. You can give the weekend a theme like 'beach getaway' or 'mountain adventure' so they know how to pack. Around 3 p.m., have a bon voyage party where everyone celebrates whatever the big milestone is. As the grand prize, three names are drawn out of a hat for an all-expenses-paid weekend trip away. The winning employees are chauffeured and the adventure begins!

Surprise Destination

Hold a surprise staff meeting away from the office. Don't tell anyone where it is going to be. When the day comes, blindfold all the participants, take a bus, and surprise them when you arrive. Another way to do this is to design a scavenger hunt where employees have to break up into teams and follow the clues provided to find the surprise destination.

Birthday Juggle

Hire a juggler or a street performer to come in for a short performance to surprise the birthday boy or girl. You can put an ad in Craigslist that you are looking for a performer. The ad might read, "I'm looking for someone who can perform a five to ten minute juggling or magic act in my office as a surprise for one of my coworkers for his/her birthday. Anytime between 3 p.m. and 5 p.m. on _____ works. My budget is small. I only need a few minutes and would even take a student who is practicing their craft. Please call_____ or email _____."

Candy Detective

Find out your co-worker's favorite candy. For one week, go undercover to hide his or her favorite candy somewhere in the office, a briefcase, or wherever is appropriate. Your coworker will appreciate snacking on a favorite treat while they try and figure out where it is coming from.

Pass the Balloons

Print customized balloons and give them away to customers and employees to celebrate different milestones. Balloons tend to make everyone a little more lighthearted and make every occasion a celebration to remember. This is a simple, easy way to honor those that matter.

Let Them Eat Cake

A sure-fire way to add celebration to any party is to bring a specially decorated cake. Whatever little or big milestone you're celebrating, bake or bring a cake and make sure to get creative with the slogan and prop on top. Have fun being silly and getting creative with what's on the cake.

Santa's Helper

Want to ease stress around the holidays and show gratitude to your staff? Surprise your employees by bringing in a holiday shopping helper. Each employee gets to come up with a list of three people they need to shop for and some ideas on what to buy them. Santa's helper sneaks off to shop with a smart phone in hand so they can take photos or Skype back to the office to confirm the gifts are appropriate before purchasing. This will pay big rewards. Employees won't be so stressed during holiday season and they won't be sneaking off to shop during business hours.

Be Late for Something Day

On the night before September 5th, tell your staff to come into work an hour late the next morning. This will be a lovely surprise for employees to have a little extra time in the morning just to celebrate Be Late for Something Day. If they are on a fixed schedule in the morning dropping off kids or spouses, then let them come back from lunch a little bit late.

Rewards on Hand

Don't be afraid to reach for whatever is near in order to reward an innovative idea or decision in the moment. Catching people doing something right and rewarding on the spot will definitely leave an impression on your employees. At the Foxborough Corporation in Massachusetts, an engineer was rewarded with a banana from the boss because it's what was readily available. This morphed into a fun award called The Golden Banana Award for invention and innovation. You never know where the best traditions and rituals may come from in your company.

Summer Brainstorming Walk

On a warm summer afternoon, surprise employees with an impromptu walk around the block. On the walk, brainstorm ideas on how to have more fun in the workplace or any other topic of value. The fresh air will rejuvenate minds and the ideas that come out of this are likely to be a breath of fresh air as well.

Surprise

Christmas in July

Surprise co-workers with a Christmas in July party. Provide them with stockings full of Christmas candy and other small gifts. Decorate the office in full-blown Christmas decorations. The CEO or a well-loved employee dresses as Santa Claus and everyone gets to take a photo on his lap. For those who don't celebrate Christmas, this is a good chance to see what all the Christmas fuss is about.

Hawaii in the Winter Day

Winters in the Northern Hemisphere can seem to go on forever. What better way to beat the chill than to have a Hawaiian-themed day in the winter? Play Hawaiian music. Bring leis. Provide fresh fruit, and chocolate macadamia nuts. Hire dancers or learn a few Hawaiian dancers and have a true Hawaiian celebration in the office.

Surprise

Easter Treats

Around Easter time, put candy, money, small toys, or clues in eggs and hide them throughout the office. Whoever collects the most eggs by the end of the day is the winner. Whether Christian or not, employees are sure to consider it a fun way to celebrate with those that are and have a good time too.

Welcome Spring

Honor spring fever on a beautiful, sunny day with a surprise outdoor picnic. Employees always appreciate a chance to enjoy the outdoors as well as a free lunch!

Post It Party

Write down as many nice things as you can about the person or team you are celebrating and start posting away. Post the notes on a computer monitor, filing cabinet, a map on the wall, or anywhere on the unsuspected recipient's desk or cubicle. It's a great way to celebrate a five or ten year anniversary, a completed project, employee appreciation day, or just because.

Surprise

Afternoon Delight

A little surprise in the afternoon may be just what the productivity doctor ordered! On the desk of a stressed employee, consider dropping off two movie passes to a recently released comedy, tickets to an art exhibit, their favorite cookie, or coffee or anything high on their joy list that would make them smile.

Pause for Applause

A memorable way to celebrate a recently finished big project is to send a memo to everyone in the company to stand up and applaud at a certain time in the afternoon. A countdown from ten to make sure everyone is with you is helpful. Scream, hoot, and holler for a minute or two to really make a big deal out of whatever you are celebrating!

A Cubicle of Epic Decorations

Surprise an honored employee by transforming his/her cubicle or office into a celebration zone. Some suggestions for decorating the space include filling it with the employee's favorite snacks, covering it with different colors and themes, or copying fun photos from their Facebook and posting them everywhere! Get creative and have some fun creating a celebration zone with the other co-workers.

Scrub-A-Dub-Dub

After a long week, hire a car washer to clean all the cars in the employee parking lot so their car is fresh and ready for the weekend. Employees will think of you all weekend long as they appreciate their clean new wheels.

Surprise

A Gift...just because...

Next time you travel, wrap a little gift for a person you haven't met yet. At some point during your trip you'll inevitably experience a special connection with someone new. Present the gift to this person and explain that you bring along a special memento on each trip knowing that you are going to meet someone special. It's a guaranteed special moment for both parties and sure to lift the spirits of the chosen gift recipient.

I learned this from my friend Debbie Taylor (www.Taylormadeevents.com) whose nicely wrapped gift is a memento from her home state of Colorado. It's usually either a John Fielder photo book with beautiful scenes of Colorado or a box of famous Enstrom's toffee.

Thanks Debbie!

Shirt the Issue

Gather a group of the more creatively inclined members of your staff to create company t-shirts. Or, have a contest for the best design. Give the t-shirts out as a surprise at the end of a busy month or to kick off a new project.

Lunch is on Us

Find out where a deserving employee is going to lunch and make arrangements for the bill to be paid. Don't let him/her know who paid for it. It's a nice way to say thank you anonymously.

Magical Chairs

Before a potentially stressful or tense employee meeting, randomly tape small gift certificates to the bottom of chairs and surprise employees with this thoughtful gift. Employees will start to look forward to those staff meetings.

Piñata Break

In the middle of a particularly stressful day, hang up a few piñatas full of candy, gift cards, or other special treats. Hitting a piñata and reaping the rewards is a wonderful way to get rid of pent up stress and anxiety.

Surprise 'no Meeting' Party

Tell your staff that there will be a very important meeting on a particular day. After everyone files in prepared for a serious meeting, yell, "Gotcha!" Turn on some music. Break out the food, and give prizes to everyone.

Room with a View

Ask employees what their favorite vacation spot is. Then, on a certain day, surprise them with a picture of their favorite place for their office. You can even take it up a notch and involve their families in order to get a picture of them at that location or superimpose them into the photo.

Two Truths and a Lie

If you have a group of new people, play this fun game in order to get to know each other better. Have each person write down two surprising facts about themselves along with a lie. Everyone else has to guess which statement is a lie. There are sure to be some funny surprises in this game!

Celebrity Kudos

Print out photos of famous celebrities and attach a make-believe greeting from the celebrity to the staff for their fine work. Personalize it for individual staff members to make it even more meaningful and fun.

Magic Of The Moment

A quick magic or card trick is always a nice way to lighten up any tense meeting or a stressful afternoon. How about an amateur magic show one afternoon at the office?

Minute to Win It

In the middle of a stressful day, have an impromptu *Minute to Win It* contest. Design easy, quick games where staff can compete against each other. This surprise break will get the competitive juices flowing and serve as a rejuvenating break.

Breakfast with the Family

Take note of an employee's special dates in life such as anniversaries, birthdays, and children's birthdays. On that day, coordinate with the employee's spouse or family and set up a surprise at a nearby restaurant. It'll be even a nicer treat when you pick up the breakfast tab.

Go for the Gold

Buy those fun chocolate gold coins and surprise workers with gold coins for a job well done. You can make it cheesy and silly by getting creative with what you say to them when you give them the coins like, "You are worth your weight in gold!"

Treat of the Month

Host a surprise treat day once a month where you honor employees with the treat of the month. Rent a popcorn or cotton candy machine or hire an ice cream cart or brick oven pizza on wheels. Krispy Crème donuts is always a good choice! Employees will always look forward to the treat of the month no matter how big or small.

Surprise

Game Day Surprise

If there is a popular sports team among the
employees in your office, hire the mascot or
someone dressed as the mascot to come to the
office and pump everyone up on a big game
day! The mascot can pass out candy. Better yet,
have the mascot pass out two free tickets to the
game for one lucky employee.

Movie Time

After finishing a big project, surprise a
department or team with movie tickets to be
used immediately during the work day.
It's a wonderful way to acknowledge a job well
done and take a little time off to unwind.

What's Behind Box #3?

Wrap all sizes of gifts in big boxes and have a celebration where employees get to choose their gift. Pick the choosing order based on longevity in the organization, closest birthday or however else you'd like. The most honored person picks lasts. The first person chooses their box, opens it up, and it will be their gift - but most likely not for long. The second person can either open a new box or take the gift from the first person at which time the first person would open a new gift. Play this way until all gifts are chosen.

A Soda or a Beer in Your Honor

Microbreweries will often brew a small run of beer and personalize it with a label with your employee's name on it. Magnificent Tim Mathy Ale is an example. You can create a label yourself and stick it over their favorite beverage. Do this as part of a ceremony or an employee appreciation event.

King or Queen for a Day

Buy a gaudy, huge, royalty-type crown and crown your king or queen for a day during a morning meeting. The king's or queen's privileges may include prime parking, free lunch at their desk, afternoon surprises, and/or the option to leave thirty minutes early from work.

Come up with your own criteria for how you choose the king or queen and have some fun with how to honor him/her.

Flex Your Time

Let go of the traditional work week. Have team members come in to work based on what works best for them. Embrace your employees' natural rhythm and commitments at home. They'll show up to work fresh and ready to go feeling appreciated for your understanding attitude.

Book It

Choose a beneficial book to your managers. Give them fifteen minutes a day to read at work. Set a finish line for when the book must be complete and then have a discussion about the book and how it can positively impact the company. Adopt the principles that make the most sense to your organization.

Surprise

Ethnic Food Festival

Honor the diversity of your staff by hosting a food festival once a quarter. Encourage staff to bring in a traditional food or snack based on their heritage or ethnicity. This is a great way to get to know your employees on a more personal level and try some delicious foods!

Lunch 'N Learn

Bring in an expert of something to hold a class for your staff on the topics they most want to hear about during lunch one day. The class could be anything from a lesson on mastering Photoshop to cooking Thai food. Staff will have a great time and enjoy the lunch provided by the company.

Favorite Movie Character Day

Take your staff to the movies in the middle of a work day. Add a little pizzazz by rolling out the red carpet as a walkway into the movie. Have popcorn bags printed with your logo and a thank you message on them. Employees will welcome a little down time after a busy period of work. Have employees dress for the experience as if they were movie characters or attending a movie premier. Hire a photographer to take pictures as they enter the movie. Award prizes for most interesting attire. Post pictures or create a PowerPoint for the next staff meeting.

Well-Manicured Office

Surprise your staff with a day of manicures around the office. Hire a team of nail technicians to come in and take care of the hands that take care of business. Not only is it a nice gesture, but it will create some good-natured kidding around how nice the men's hands look as well!

Birthday Takeover

Celebrate the birthday of a co-worker by taking over as many of their daily tasks as possible. Perform the tasks like you're the lead concierge at the Four Seasons Hotel. Sprinkle a few gifts along the way. Hide some Post-It notes with nice comments on their desk, and surprise them with their favorite snack.

Flash Mob

Surprise an unsuspecting employee by honoring him/her with a personal flash mob. It takes less time than you think for the staff to learn a dance. The payoffs are big. What a fun way to engage and connect a team or department while learning a fun dance to surprise a treasured employee. Start here: www.wikihow.com/Organize-a-Flash-Mob

Cast a Spell on You

Stage a spelling bee in-office with prizes for the top three spots. You'll see the employees stir up a firestorm in their heads by guessing and spelling those tough words we don't use often. Employees can contribute words to the competition and don't be surprised if employees actually learn something in the process.

What A Character

Challenge your employees to draw a caricature of a co-worker. Encourage them to at least try to scribble something and exaggerate or make up those prominent features like maybe that duck tail mustache, hawk nose, or weird hairstyle. Let the best resemblance be awarded.
Have a guessing game. People try to guess the person in the caricature.

Play Ball in The House

Indoor bowling can be played on any fairly flat surface of your office, and you can use any space like the cafeteria, a conference room, or even the hallways between cubicles.

Hire out the bowling equipment and nominate one employee to act as the referee.

Duct Tape Day

Bring in multiple rolls of different colored and designed duct tape. Make projects out of the duct tape as a fun stress relief exercise. Search 'ductivities' on the web for some inspiration. Have a little competition for the most creative or useful duct tape creation.

Surprise

Hide And Wait

Hide a photo or memento in a co-worker's office. See how long it takes for him/her to notice. This is a fun way to remind staff of the power of surprise.

Financial Checkup

Bring in financial experts. Offer one hour estate planning, free investment advice, and tax or budgeting help. Employees will appreciate the free assistance.

Leaving on a Jet Plane

Need a little stress relief in the office? Design and host an in-office paper airplane contest. Employees will have a blast designing the best paper airplane and competing against each other. The winner of the competition can get a small prize, like an extra thirty minutes for lunch, or a big prize, like some frequent flyer miles to be used for their next vacation.

Military Care from the Company

Put together care packages during special occasions or holidays. Send to those serving in the military. The employees are sure to enjoy giving back and doing some good for others.

Handy Man Birthday

Hire a handy man to perform maintenance work at the home of an employee celebrating a birthday that week. If nothing needs fixing, hire someone to mow the employee's lawn or a service to tidy up the house.

Comical Spill

Have all the employees write their favorite joke on note cards. Put them up in the break room or kitchen. It's a simple gesture that will surely encourage your staff to make sure they are taking time to laugh throughout the work day.

Ditch the Formal Reviews

Netflix encourages its managers and employees to have conversations about performance as an organic part of their work. By making employee performance a topic of regular conversation you can alleviate the stress that formal reviews bring to the office.

Hobby Pay

Reward a job well done by giving your hardworking employee something that supports a favorite hobby. This might be a set of paint brushes for the avid artist or a new recipe book for the employee who loves to cook. By learning more about your employees and rewarding them with what's highest on their joy list, you will further develop and increase positivity in your working relationship.

Bucket Brigade

Have each of your staff turn in a bucket list. Look for opportunities to help your staff achieve dreams. When a major goal is achieved, reward an honorary employee with the resources needed to check off an item from that list.

Do the Doodle

Designate one wall in the office for doodles. Get sticky tape to post them all over the wall. Periodically, hold a judging contest for the best doodle and award that person with a fresh doodle pad and pencils. This is a simple way to increase creativity in the office.

We Should Take This Outside!

The meeting that is! On a nice day, hold your regularly scheduled meeting outside with lemonade or iced tea. Your staff will appreciate some time away from the office to enjoy the outdoors. Don't forget the sunscreen!

Select an All-Star

During All-Star voting for either Major League Baseball or the National Football League, have a voting session at work for your very own 'office all-star'. The employee with the most votes gets two free tickets to a MLB or NFL game. Get creative in making your own criteria for what makes a great 'office all-star.'

Baby Bonds

Showcase appreciation and gratitude for employees by acknowledging those important milestones in life. Buy savings bonds for the newborn children and grandchildren of your staff. It's a wonderful gesture and the employee will surely be grateful for it.

Take out The Baby

At Google, new mothers and fathers get something called 'Take-Out Benefits' to help make things easier. These employees are provided with expenses up to $500 for take-out meals during the first three months that they are home with their new baby. Feel free to get creative in developing a different way to offer your support and care to staff members during this time.

Showcase Your Staff

Make it a point to learn about your staff's hobbies and pastimes. If your staff members have interesting hobbies like quilting, building muscle cars, or painting, allow them an opportunity for a gallery-type show in the office. Make it a fun event by inviting friends, providing snacks, and allowing employees to take a bit of a social break.

Surprise

Help Your Work Neighbor

Ask employees to draw names out of a hat for
the co-worker for whom they will have to be a
"work neighbor helper." The duty of the work
neighbor is to help the person selected with
something outside of the office.
Perhaps they need a babysitter for an evening
or would like some help around the yard.
Whatever it is, employees will feel great about
being their new "work neighbor's helper.
It is a great way to get to know one another
better. The "work neighbor helper" can hire
a babysitter or handyman with approval
of the neighbor, of course.

Summer Break

In the summer time, how about giving two
Fridays a month off? Employees will be so
elated at the opportunity to start their
summer weekends a day early that
productivity will be sure to rise.

Applause! Applause!

Physically applaud your people by giving them a round of applause for specific achievements. Where? When? The answer is wherever and whenever. You can applaud a special, hardworking employee at meetings or company-sponsored social gatherings, a luncheon, or in the office. It will be even better if you create you own special clap when applauding that becomes recognized as the clap of appreciation.

Calendar Keeper

Create a social calendar or events board so employees can link up for activities after work. Keep it in a central location with all of the details of the events attached. Post envelopes around the calendar for a place to put invitations to special events so anyone can grab one! This is a great way to assist the staff in bonding outside of work.

Surprise

Charitable Donations

Ask employees to identify their favorite causes and charities. When an employee finishing a great project or puts in that extra effort, make a charitable donation in their name. It doesn't have to be a big donation, just something that lets that employee know you care about their causes and recognize their hard work.

Recognition Box

Put a recognition box in a central area. Leave plenty of cards, sticky notes, and stickers there ready for action. Acknowledge those employees who congratulate and thank their co-workers.

Unusual Holiday

Create a silly holiday card for an employee on a day when you wouldn't normally give a holiday card. Some examples of holidays that don't typically use cards are April Fools' Day, President's Day, or even International Bald Person's Day. There's a plethora of them. It's just a fun excuse to let someone know you're thinking about him or her and that you care. My Halloween and April Fools' Day cards get a lot of positive feedback!

Surprise

Guest Chef for The Day

After your team has accomplished a milestone or worked extra long hours, consider hiring a friend who is a great cook to come into the office and prepare a special meal for them. If you have an employee who is a great cook, why not give him/her time to do this?

Secret Admirer

Send a deserving employee roses or a box of chocolates with a note that compliments him or her on something that deserves mentioning. Sign the note anonymously as that employee's secret admirer.

Mail Surprises

Every now and then, hide gift certificates or funny notes in the daily mail. Big stacks of mail can be a seemingly endless chore to employees. Transform this boring task into a fun one as employees go through the daily mail hoping for a surprise.

The Treat Man

Find out the favorite snack of each individual team member. When you catch them doing something right, reward them with this treat. Don't do it more than once a week or it will become stale fast, but an occasional special treat will continue to show that you're paying attention.

Impromptu Outings

After a hectic project or a big achievement, surprise the team with a trip to an ice cream store, coffee cafe, or even a bowling alley. A short, small outing is a wonderful way to give thanks and show gratitude for a job well done.

Surprise Picnic for Two

Cater a delicious, fun picnic lunch for a special employee on a nice, warm day. Surprise him/her by inviting the spouse or significant other along on this extra-long lunch.

Collect Collectors' Collections

Discover what your team members' hobbies or collections are and throughout the year add a special piece to that collection. During special times or after a milestone has been met, present the collectors' item to the collector. Stamps, coins, dolls, and spoons are always a big hit to the collectors of those items.

Dinner with the Boss

Contact the spouse of an employee you'd like to recognize and set up a dinner at the guest of honor's favorite restaurant. Have the spouse make up a story about whom they're having dinner with. When they show up, it will really be a surprise to have dinner with the boss and his/her spouse. It's an honor to have dinner with the boss and will show that you care about spending one-on-one, personal time with deserving employees. Consider making it a family dinner.

Surprise Holiday Party

Pick a holiday, any holiday, in which the company is still working. In the afternoon, throw a surprise party with a fun band and some delicious treats to snack on. Employees always appreciate a little break from work, especially on holidays.

Puzzled

Want to award someone who has solved a problem spontaneously or who acted as a master problem solver? Surprise them with a puzzle that has some significance. For example, you can turn a favorite photo into a puzzle that features a favorite hobby or sports team.

Cookie Monster

Early in the afternoon when employees need a little pick me up, drop off a cookie on each employee's desk. No note. No announcement. Surprise! If you can do your homework ahead of time and find out favorite cookie flavors, the impact will be even greater.

Lights, Camera, Action!

Surprise your staff with an in-house movie marathon. Set up a theatre in the boardroom. Show popular old classics or themed movies. Don't forget the popcorn and snacks. It's a great way to say thank you for a busy period of hard work and give them some much needed break time.

Tap into the Treasury

Surprise your workers with rare coins or bills for their efforts. Susan B. Anthony Dollars or a $2 bill would be a special treat in the U.S. as you don't see them in circulation. Do you have a currency or coin in your country that would be a nice surprise and reward? Check out sources online or at your bank.

Sorry Surprise

If you are late delivering on a commitment, make it a little easier to accept with a surprise reward. One way to do this is to attach a candy bar or a free frozen yogurt certificate on top of a late report. It is a good way to ease the tension of the receiver. However, don't use this as a strategy to be late with commitments. It's much better to deliver on what is promised.

Chocolate Your Way

Celebrate an employee by letting him/her order a box of favorites. Even better, play chocolate detective and find out exactly what they want and surprise them. On the See's Candies website, www.sees.com, you can easily customize your very own box of chocolates. You can do this for Valentine's Day, their birthday, or create your very own special holiday.

Surprise

Secret Saying Poster

Make a list of your favorite quotes and have the employees do the same. Gather all the lists of quotes and print them out on bright, colorful slips of paper. Post them on the wall of your department's office or all over the cubicles.

Celebration Buddy Month

During February, each person draws a name of a celebration buddy and for one month, they provide surprises for their buddy while keeping their identity secret. Encourage them to provide at least one surprise per week. The purpose of this exercise is to help bring joy into the life of their celebration buddy. This is guaranteed to raise the morale level of any organization while they try and figure out who their celebration buddy is.

Go the Extra Mile for a Milestone

Make a big deal out of career accomplishments, new babies in the family, or marriage anniversaries. Personalized coffee mugs and t-shirts with fun photos on them presented at a quick ceremony during the day are a nice touch and will make a difference to the employee.

Undercover Agent

Have a secret team of employees who have one purpose… to delightfully surprise other employees. They choose the criteria on who will be surprised and how. It may be a little gift wrapped box at 3 pm that when opened instructs them to meet at the copy machine at 4 PM to make a copy of the enclosed document. When they go to make a copy there is an envelope taped to the machine with their name on it containing two passes to their favorite comedian to town.

One of a Kind

Appoint the Kindness Patrol to catch people being kind and reward them with gift cards from Amazon, Starbucks, and their favorite store. Kind workplaces are happier workplaces.

Wall of Good

Create a wall for the purpose of letting your employees post photos of charity work they have done. If your company is involved with Habitat for Humanity or Professionals without Borders, this would be a great opportunity to share your good work with all staff. It will remind people what's most important in life.

Now It's Up to You

There you have it—365 ways to add a little more celebration to your workplace! If my math is correct, that would be one celebration a day. So now what do you do?

It would sure help to have the support of your organization's leaders as well as HR, but it won't always happen. If you focus on using the ideas in this book in your organization, little by little, the GPS Celebration mentality will spread. Engage other champions from different departments and in time, you'll notice a positive difference.

By turning on your personal GPS and your organization's GPS, you will create a happier, healthier workplace... one celebration at a time.

Scott's Programs

"Celebrate! Lessons Learned from the World's Most Admired Organizations"

"Celebration" is one of the most effective ways to engage employees, improve team performance, and raise productivity. In this entertaining, interactive, content-rich session, you will learn how to create a culture of celebration leading to more innovative, authentic, responsive employees. Learn what the most admired organizations are doing to honor, celebrate, engage, and retain employees and customers. Your reward will be a happier, healthier, more engaged workplace.

"The Best Way to Predict the Future Is to Create It"

In these globally competitive times, resourcefulness and innovation are essential to survival. This program is a fast-paced, humorous call-to-action that will show your attendees how to become a victor—rather than a victim—of change. They will learn to be driven not by circumstances and emotions, but by purpose and values. Scott's easy-to-use ideas will help build more team spirit, greater productivity, elevated team performance, and a happier, healthier culture. This program is an ideal kick-off or closing. It always leaves participants feeling energized, inspired, and more accountable to create a better future for themselves and their organizations!

"Connecting with Customers"

Customer expectations have dramatically changed over the years. Today, satisfying the needs of your customers by providing fast, efficient service is no longer enough. The most successful companies move beyond customer satisfaction and engage customers in a memorable experience that is consistent with their brand promise. Every employee must take pride in a service culture that honors and rewards both employees and customers. This entertaining and insightful program will help you establish a deeper connection with your employees and customers, leading to better team performance, higher productivity, and more loyal customers. You will find that connected employees create connected customers.

"Using Humor for a Change"

Become unforgettable. Jump-start your creativity. Ease conflict. Gain control of tense situations. Win impossible business. Create a positive culture. Engage employees. Engage customers. Reduce burnout. Improve communication. Enhance problem solving. Build better relationships. Raise productivity... and enjoy work more than ever before! How do you make this happen? Through the effective use of humor in the workplace. This lively, interactive program explores ways to use humor, creativity, and engagement strategies to bring more positivity and productivity to your organization. You will learn to tap into your unique sense of humor—a skill essential in building deeper relationships and better results. By using the tools from this fun, useful program, you will soon discover that those who laugh, last!

"Sell-e-brate! Winning the Hearts and Business of Tomorrow's Customers"

This useful and entertaining program explores how to use celebration, humor, and value-adding creativity to give your sales team a competitive advantage. These important tools, along with the "Sell-e-brate Mindset," will help generate new clients and keep your existing customer base consistently engaged and satisfied. By creating a culture of celebration and honoring your employees and customers, you will create happy, eager prospects ready to buy. Learn ways to differentiate yourself and build perceived value that highlights what you do best. Let your "GPS"—Gratitude, Play, and Surprise—guide you to better connections with customers, leading to the discovery of hidden objections. As you learn techniques used by the world's most admired organizations, you will discover that he or she who celebrates, sells!

"Employee Innovation in Turbulent Times"

What does it take to stay relevant and competitive in today's fast-paced, ever-changing global marketplace? A culture of innovation! In fact, the #1 killer of employee innovation is a culture that does not support it. Employees are more mobile, versatile, and appreciate their personal freedom more than any time in the history of work. The needs and demands of today's workforce make the task of employee engagement more complicated. When self-expression is welcomed, when employees feel free to be authentic, when employees are empowered to take risks, when creativity is rewarded—innovation flourishes. A connected culture leads employees to brainstorm, create, and thrive. Learn to build a culture that engages employees, creates connections, and lets employees know that what they do matters. Your reward will be more productive, creative, and fulfilled employees.

"How to Hold an Audience without a Rope"

To be a great leader, you must be a great communicator, and to be a great communicator, you must speak with clarity, power, and purpose. The best speakers build perceived credibility through authentic vulnerability, humility, and the art of storytelling. In this program you will learn the secrets of great speakers from the conference room to the podium. You'll learn how to overcome stage fright, establish perceived credibility, and create an authentic connection with your listeners. Your value as a leader will dramatically increase as you learn to hold an audience without a rope.

"Happily Ever Laughter"

To truly engage the distracted audience member of today, you must not only educate and enlighten, but entertain as well. Humor may be your most useful tool for it breaks preoccupation, develops rapport, increases retention, and connects with your listeners. In this interactive skill-shop, participants will learn how to play off any audience—be it a meeting of five or an auditorium of 5,000. From developing original material to uncovering an organization's "humor hot buttons," this program will cover the basics and beyond for become a more charismatic, humorous, effective presenter. Learn to tell funny stories that appeal to a culturally diverse audience. From "half-the-words" to "what if" to the "power of the pause," you will learn story-telling techniques that will make your stories come alive.

To order, or for more information,
please contact us:

www.ScottFriedman.net
e-mail: Scott@ScottFriedman.net
+1-303-284-0811
16351 West Ellsworth Avenue,
Golden, CO 80401
USA

Manufactured by Amazon.ca
Bolton, ON

34056273R00087